Patterns

Peter Patilla

Heinemann Library
Des Plaines, Illinois

Designed by AMR
Illustrations by Art Construction and Jessica Stockham (Beehive Illustration)
Originated by HBM Print Ltd, Singapore
Printed and bound by South China Printing Co., Hong Kong/China

04 03 02 01 00
10 9 8 7 6 5 4 3 2

Library of Congress Cataloging-in-Publication Data

Patilla, Peter.
    Patterns / Peter Patilla.
        p. cm. – (Math links)
    Includes bibliographical references and index.
    Summary: Explores the mathematical concept of patterns as with sequence and repetition, and including patterns found in nature, color, and line, as well as number patterns, symmetrical patterns, and tessellating patterns.
    ISBN 1-57572-967-9 (lib. bdg.)
    1. Pattern perception Juvenile literature. [1. Pattern perception.] I. Title. II. Series: Patilla, Peter. Math links.
BF311.P3155 1999
510—dc21   99-24955
                                                   CIP

Acknowledgments
The Publishers would like to thank the following for permission to reproduce photographs:
Trevor Clifford, pp. 8, 15, 17, 22, 24, 25, 26, 28; Bruce Coleman Ltd./Luiz Claudio Marigo, p. 4; Bruce Coleman Ltd./Kim Taylor, p. 27; Bruce Coleman Ltd./Dr. Stephen Coyne, p. 29; Oxford Scientific Films/F. J. Hiersche/Okapia, p. 6; Science Photo Library/Adam Hart-Davis, p. 7; Science Photo Library/Peter Menzel, p. 11; Science Photo Library/Martin Dohrn, p. 21; Stockfile/Steven Behr, p. 18; Tony Stone Images/David Sutherland, p. 10; Tony Stone Images/Jean Françoise Causse, p. 13.

Cover photo: Trevor Clifford

Our thanks to David Kirkby for his comments in the preparation of this book.

Every effort has been made to contact copyright holders of any material reproduced in this book. Any omissions will be rectified in subsequent printings if notice is given to the Publisher.

Some words in this book are in bold, **like this.** You can find out what they mean by looking in the glossary. Look for the answers to the questions in the green boxes on page 32.

Contents

Animal Patterns

Some animals have special patterns on their bodies. These patterns are often stripes or spots. The pattern of colors and shapes makes it difficult to see the animal. The pattern is a **camouflage**.

4

The patterns help the animals hide in long grass or among stones. The colors help the animals blend with the background colors.

Which animals might have the patterns shown on this page?

Nature's Patterns

Patterns can be seen all around us. Patterns can be found on seashells, flowers, and birds. They can be in the colors, the shapes, and the **textures**. Nature has many wonderful patterns.

Plants have different kinds of patterns. The veins on a leaf make a pattern. The pattern helps us to know which tree the leaf comes from.

Look at the leaves. Which leaves might come from the same tree?

Printed Patterns

Patterns can be printed. The pattern can be **repeated** many times. This picture shows printed fingerprint patterns. Each person in the world has a **unique** fingerprint pattern.

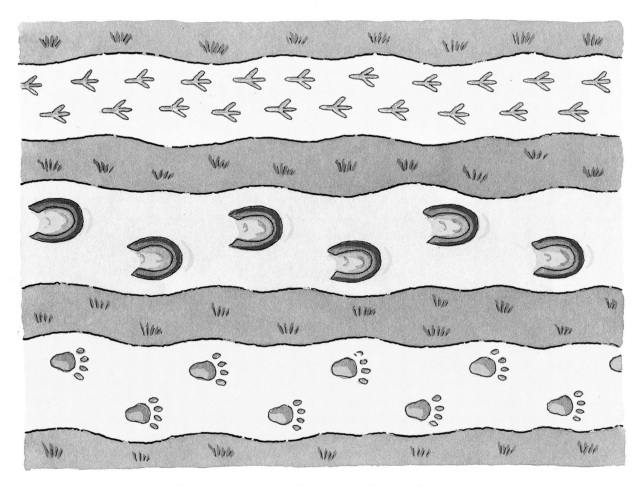

The shapes of animals' feet often leave patterns on the ground. These are footprint patterns. Each kind of animal leaves a different footprint.

Which animals might make the footprint patterns on this page?

Color Patterns

Colors can make patterns, too. Sometimes the pattern has different shades of one color, such as light blue and dark blue. These are called **tints**, or hues, of blue.

10

A rainbow always makes a pattern of seven colors. The colors are red, orange, yellow, green, blue, indigo, and violet. Each color gently blends into the color next to it.

Look at this picture of a rainbow. Find each of the seven colors.

Line Patterns

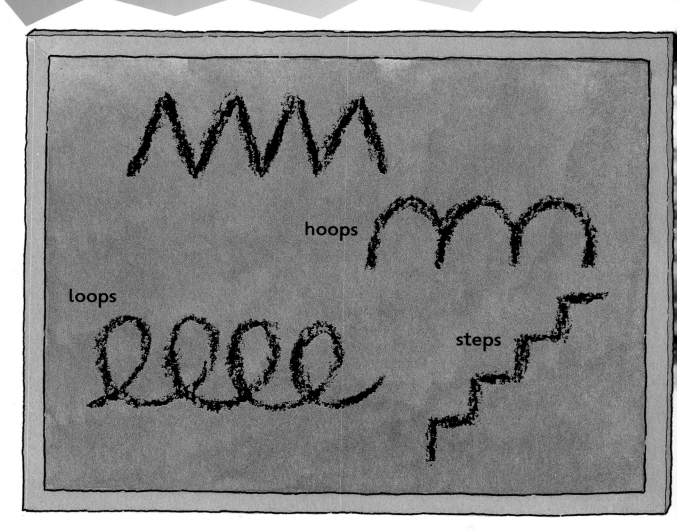

Lines can be drawn to make patterns. The lines can be straight or **curved**. Line patterns can look like zigzags, loops, steps, or hoops.

Line patterns can be found all around us.

Sometimes they are made by people.

Sometimes they are made by animals or nature.

Look for the line patterns in the picture.

Spirals

Spirals can have **curved** or straight lines. Spiral lines can wind out from the center. Spiral lines can wind around and around like a **coil** of rope.

14

The spirals on these screws end in a point. The spirals on the bolts stop at a flat end.

How many spirals can you see in the picture?

Repeating Patterns

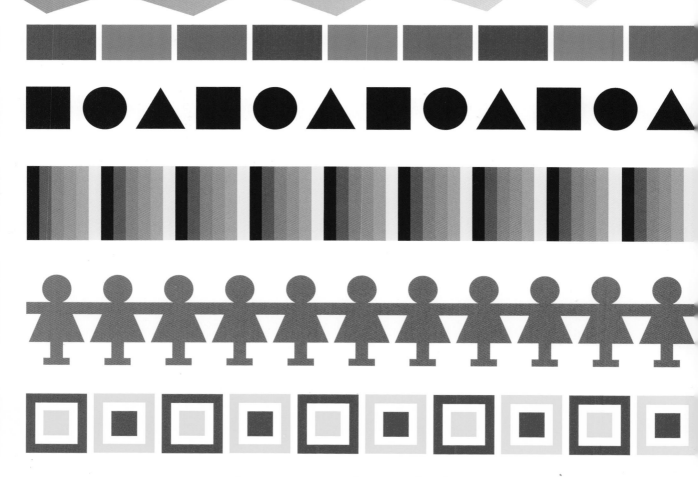

A **sequence** is how one thing follows another.

It can be the order in which something happens.

It can be the order of pictures or objects in a line.

Sequences can make **repeating** patterns.

Repeating patterns are all around us. Sometimes they happen naturally. Sometimes people make them happen.

Repeating patterns are found in fabric designs.

Ring Patterns

Some patterns go around in a ring. These are called **ring patterns**. Shapes, colors, or lines might make a ring pattern.

18

Ring patterns can be found all around us. A pattern is **repeated** to form the ring.

What pattern is repeated to make the ring in each picture on this page?

Overlapping Patterns

When shapes **overlap**, they are on top of each other. When the center of each shape is in the same place, the shapes are **concentric**. Overlapping and concentric shapes can form patterns.

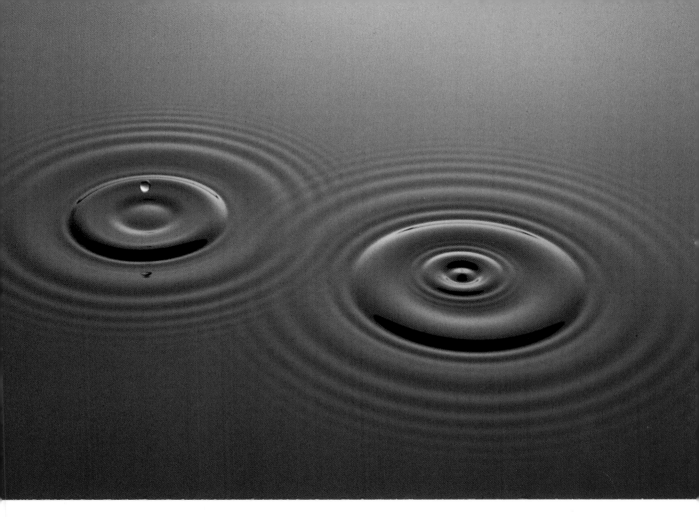

A bull's-eye target has concentric circles of different colors. When a tree has been cut down, we can see the concentric growth rings inside.

A stone dropped into water makes ripples. The ripples are concentric circles.

Stacking Patterns

Things are often **stacked** in a pattern. Sometimes the things are stacked together in a tight pattern. Other times there are spaces between the things in the pattern.

Bricklayers put bricks in patterns. They can make many different patterns. Sometimes a brick pattern has spaces between the bricks.

How many different brick patterns are there in the picture on this page?

Number Patterns

Numbers of things can be arranged to make patterns. An **even number** of things can be put into a pattern of twos. An **odd number** of things cannot be put into a pattern of twos.

Counting things is easier when they are in a pattern. Sometimes when we see the pattern, we do not have to count each thing.

The dots on the cubes are arranged in patterns. How many dots are on each cube?

Symmetrical Patterns

The mirror shows a **reflection** of a puddle of paint. The reflection and the puddle look the same. The reflection and the puddle make a **symmetrical** pattern.

There are many symmetrical patterns in nature.
The pattern on the butterfly's right wing is just
like the pattern on its left wing.

When you fold a shape in the middle, it is
symmetrical if the two halves match.

Tessellating Patterns

Some patterns use small squares or blocks that are very close together. This is a **tessellating** pattern. A tessellating pattern can be **symmetrical,** too.

28

From earliest times, people have made **mosaics.**
Mosaic pictures are made by tessellating pieces
of tile or glass. Mosaics decorate floors, walls,
windows, and ceilings.

Tile floors are tessellating patterns. Where else
can you find tessellations?

Glossary

camouflage disguise that blends into the background color or pattern

coil wound around in rings

concentric having the same center

curved line that is not straight

even number number of things that can be put into pairs without any left over; 2, 4, 6, 8, 10 are even numbers

identical same shape and size

mosaic picture made of small pieces of stone, glass, or wood fitted together

overlap something placed on top of something else

odd number number of things that cannot be put into pairs without having one left over; 1, 3, 5 ,7 ,9 are odd numbers

reflection what you see in a mirror

repeating happening more than once

ring pattern **sequence** that forms a circle

sequence order of something

spiral line that winds around and widens out from a center

stack orderly pile

symmetrical shape or picture that is balanced on both sides of a line

tessellating pattern with parts that touch each other

texture look or feel of something

tint shade of a color, such as dark blue or light pink

unique nothing else is like it; one of a kind

More Books to Read

Eston, Rebeka, and Karen Economopopulos. *Pattern Trains & Hopscotch Paths: Exploring Pattern.* White Plaines, N.Y.: Seymour, Dale Publications, 1997.

Kirkby, David. *Patterns.* Crystal Lake, Ill.: Rigby Interactive Library, 1996.

Kirkby, David. *Patterns.* Crystal Lake, Ill.: Rigby Interactive Library, 1996. An older reader will help you with this book.

Pluckrose, Henry . *Pattern.* Danbury, Conn.: Children's Press, 1995.

Answers

Index